Protecting Those You Love

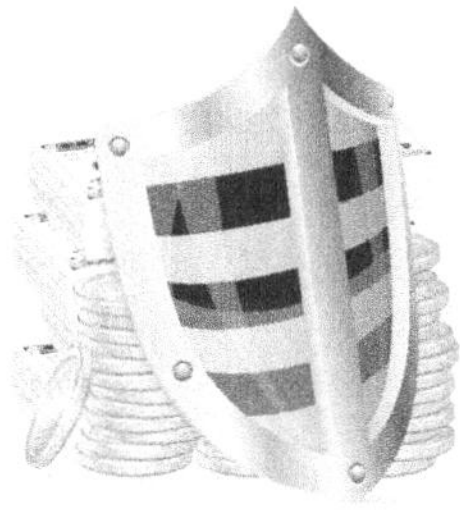

Simple Steps
To Making Your World Safer

MATT MILLER

Protecting Those You Love

ISBN: 978-1-946203-53-3

Disclaimer

This publication is designed to provide accurate and authoritative information regarding the subject matter contained within. It should be understood that the author and publisher are not engaged in rendering legal, accounting or other financial service through this medium. The author and publisher shall not be liable for your misuse of this material and shall have neither liability nor responsibility to anyone with respect to any loss or damage caused, or alleged to be caused, directly or indirectly by the information contained in this book. The author and/or publisher do not guarantee that anyone following these strategies, suggestions, tips, ideas or techniques will become successful. If legal advice or other expert assistance is required, the services of a competent professional should be sought.

Matthew G. Miller, PC, LLO
9290 W. Dodge Rd. #100
Omaha, NE 68114
(402) 558-4900

Expert Press
www.ExpertPress.net

Table of Contents

Testimonials

"I never dreamed I would need legal counsel until my husband was killed in a boating incident. I was lost as to what to do next. I knew I needed a lawyer. Matt was the first lawyer I visited. By the time I left his office, I felt comfortable and confident that Matt had my family in his best interest. I thought to be fair I should visit other lawyers. I interviewed two other lawyers and knew within minutes I was just another client to them.

Matt was personable, honest, caring and easy to talk to. He explained the options and decisions of my case thoroughly. He acted promptly and went the extra mile to help my family. When it was time to settle, I felt like I was discussing my case with a close friend. He was intelligent and knowledgeable and counseled me about what was best.

Matt helped my family and me through a very difficult time. I would refer Matt to anyone seeking professional advice."

—Kim Mahoney,
Omaha, Nebraska,
Wrongful Death Claim

"Matt has changed my life. He helped my family through the toughest times of our lives and guided us through the legal mess of my car accident. Without him I have no idea where I would be today. With his help I can now put myself through a good college and live comfortably as no one in my family has ever done. He made sure that I got the best possible outcome and always kept me very informed and up to date on what was going on with my case. I not only see him as my attorney, I see him as a friend that I can depend on and trust for anything whether it be legal advice or advice on a life problem.

Thank you Matt for everything you have done for me and I look forward to our lifelong friendship."

—Paul Ivey,
Omaha, Nebraska

"Matt was our saving grace when our son was in an accident as a passenger in a friend's car and his insurance was not enough to cover our son's medical bills. First of all, we didn't think we needed to hire an attorney, we just wanted to get the medical bills paid. The car insurance and health insurance companies were both telling us different things and neither wanted to pay for the bills first.

We met Matt and felt very comfortable with him right away. He assured us that he would handle the bill situation with the hospitals and the insurance companies and he did just that. Matt was always available to speak with when we needed him and we felt that he truly cared not only about our case, but about our son also.

Matt was able to not only get all the bills handled, but sent us to someone who sat down with our son to discuss future career/college options since the accident could alter his future work choices. This is something that we would have never thought of doing ourselves.

Because of Matt and his expertise, our son's future should be a bright one. Thank you Matt and everyone in his office who made this very difficult and scary time in our lives so much easier."

—Liz Larson,
Omaha, Nebraska

Introduction

Dear Reader,

Throughout 30 years of practicing law, I've helped people after dramatic, horrible, life-altering things have happened to them.

These experiences have shaped my desire to help others in any way possible.

My years as a lawyer have given me a unique perspective of the legal system and how our very laws that should exist to protect us may sometimes work against us. Simply put...our legal system is flawed. Large insurance companies are dictating how cases are determined in our courts. Unfortunately, the courts' rulings are often to the detriment of people seeking justice.

After 30 years, I still feel frustration, sadness, even anger when I see how insurance companies can take advantage of regular people—just like you. And I wanted to write a book that just might give you some insider knowledge that would help you protect yourself and your loved ones.

My clients are victims when they come to me, and I'm determined to help them in any way I can. If you've already been in an accident, there are certain things you can do to protect your rights. And if there is an accident awaiting you in the future—you can use these tips to prepare yourself.

Don't fall through these trap doors. Be aware of your rights. And have the materials and knowledge you need to truly protect your loved ones

This book contains a list of pointers that you can use. It is an easy reference guide of steps you can take right now—before anything happens. An accident is, by definition, unexpected. Because we don't know what the future holds, you should prepare now to protect yourself.

It is crucial to take the necessary steps in advance to try to make sure you are protected in the event of an accident.

This book is for everyone. Do you own a car? Do you have insurance? Are you the decision-maker in the family? Do you have children, a spouse, other loved ones who will be drivers (or passengers) on the road?

If you answered yes to any of these questions—you'll find useful information in this book.

So, why should you listen to me?

I've been practicing law in this area for 30 years. It's the only type of law that I've ever practiced.

For the first five years of my career, I defended the big insurance companies. And I was disturbed to learn that they were using hardball tactics in dealing with injured people. They were trying to minimize or avoid their financial responsibilities for harms or losses that their drivers caused.

That firsthand insight into their hard-nosed tactics woke me up to the real story of what happens behind the scenes.

Needless to say, I switched sides and have vigorously pursued justice and reparations on behalf of plaintiffs (injured parties) in personal injury cases ever since.

People need to be mindful of that fact that those insurance companies (even your very own insurance company to whom you pay premiums every month) are only in business for profit. They truly don't have your best interests at heart.

It's hard to hear, but it is the truth.

I think most people are good, honest, and trusting. They buy insurance and trust that the company will protect them should anything happen. But they may have a brutal awakening in their future.

The bottom line is that there is no substitute for experience. And I'd like to share my experience from what I have gleaned through all these years.

I hope you'll find this book a quick, simple and easy reference guide. And if you make these simple changes or take these easy-to-follow steps, you'll better protect yourself and your family.

If anything happens, you'll be ready.

I hope you enjoy this book and, as always, I'm here if you feel the need to reach out.

My best,

Matt Miller

SECTION ONE:

PROTECTION

Chapter 1.

The Family Business

I was born and raised in Omaha, Nebraska to a wonderful set of parents. I guess you could say that I attribute all of my success to them and the example they set for me. Loving, caring, good role models—what more could a fellow ask for?

After high school, I went to trade school to learn tool-and-die making because I've always liked working with my hands. Yes, seriously. But I was an avid reader and would often get way off topic while having discussions with my instructors.

In trade school, I had an instructor who was a former Navy Seal who had served in Vietnam. He was such an inspiration to me, and I really respected his thoughts and perspectives. This instructor told me I was not where I belonged. He encouraged me to go to a university and study.

Well, my father was a successful attorney. And I never really fully understood the whole concept of what he did for a living. While I was growing up, I knew my dad was a lawyer, but it was really just a term—not something I took personally. In addition, I had made my father a promise. He'd once told me that I could be anything I wanted in life—except a lawyer. I never knew why he made me promise this, but I'd kept my promise to this point.

I idolized my father and regularly put him on a pedestal. The last thing I ever wanted to do was to disappoint him. But, after I went to college, I spent some time with him during a break. I was able to actually observe him in court during a trial.

This was it. It lit a fire under me like no other. I knew then and there that I wanted to be a lawyer too. The only problem was that I had to confess this to my father.

When I finally admitted the truth to him, he was absolutely delighted. He explained that he hadn't wanted me to follow in his footsteps because of the stress that being a lawyer could bring into your life. He made clear that helping others obtain the truth and justice that they deserved would rest on my shoulders.

He had a sort of love/hate relationship with the practice of law. But he told me that he believed that you don't pick your career—your career picks you.

Going to law school and learning the skills needed to practice law was an eye-opener. There are far too many lawyers and not enough good ones. From my perspective, the practice of law is about service to other people. It is about giving people who have been harmed a voice and helping them obtain the justice they deserve.

I've worked hard over the past 30 years to build a team of people who share my world view and my values. People come to me after having survived a catastrophic event. They are worried about life and financial concerns. They might be injured. They may have lost a family member.

So it's a huge responsibility to go through this journey with them. They turn their case over to us and lay it on our laps. And I don't ever quit thinking about them, even when I go home at night.

At the same time, it's an incredible honor and a privilege to be trusted with this responsibility. And there is not a finer feeling in the world than to help people survive a difficult experience.

I take every case as if I'm ready to go to war and fight on behalf of my client against a skilled and well-financed opposition.

My father was a champion of the underdog, and I like to think of myself as the same. I look out for the downtrodden. This is part and parcel of who I am. I take that worry and insomnia on behalf of my clients because the payoff is an incredible sense of satisfaction when we get justice. In the end, it is all worth it.

I understand why my father chose this line of work. This is what he lived, and it is what I've lived for 30 years now.

And that's why I want to share this knowledge and experience with you—the reader. If you can learn and use at least one thing from this book, it will be a true success in my heart and mind.

Chapter 2.

Your Auto Coverage (UM/UIM)

When it comes to your auto insurance coverage, there are a few things you may not know. But, before I go into those details, I will make note here that every state has its own regulations and minimum coverage laws. So I do advise you to check on these limits for your particular state.

Automobile coverage includes something referred to as UM/UIM coverage. UM coverage means Un-insured Motorist Coverage—so someone who does not have insurance coverage. UIM coverage means Under-insured Motorist Coverage—this is someone who has insurance but the policy limits are less than they need or minimal.

Currently, in Nebraska, the minimum coverage is $25,000 per person or $50,000 per accident as a minimum.

For example: If someone runs a red light and damages multiple cars, no matter how many people were injured or how much damage was caused, the absolute most the insurance can pay out is $25,000 per person and $50,000 total per accident.

People who operate with minimum limits often have no other assets that you could possibly pursue in court. So you can unwittingly be in a bad position if a minimally insured driver causes an accident in which you or your car are involved.

In most states, to get your car registered and titled, you will have to show proof of minimum limits of coverage. But then, sometimes, these people stop making payments on insurance after they get their registration.

In fact, many people drive around with no coverage at all. And it is very common to see these irresponsible people cause wrecks.

So, if this happens, the only real protection you have is this UM/UIM coverage on your own policy. These are combined into one type of coverage, and it will compensate you and your passengers regardless of the other driver's coverage.

How much will it cost to add this coverage?

Well, I recommend that you sit down sit down with your agent and go over all of your coverages one by one. What you'll most likely find is that what really drives the cost of your coverage is the type of deductible you are applying to property damage. By adjusting the deductible amount, you should be able to easily afford adding the UM/UIM coverage to your plan.

Most people never imagine that something horrible could happen to them because they feel like a safe driver or that they will be able to avoid it.

And those people are primarily concerned with how much money they would have to pay if there's a fender-bender in the grocery store parking lot or if a tree falls on their car or if there is hail damage to their car.

But if you think about these things from a high level, and you consider all the things that can/do go wrong in life—the vehicle that you're in is the very least important thing.

At the end of the day, the car is just an object. If it is wrecked, that property damage is not going to radically alter your life or lifestyle and your ability to provide for your family.

If you adjust your property damage deductible, which may currently be as low as $250 dollars, and increase it to $1,000 or even $1,500, you will discover that the rates you have to pay will plummet. That allows you to easily increase your UM/UIM coverage.

Take a close look at your deductible. UM/UIM coverage is extremely important and something I highly recommend.

Personally, I have maxed out my UM/UIM to in the range of $250,000 to $500,000 worth of coverage. I afforded this by increasing my deductible and offsetting the cost of my policy.

This is one of the most important things you can do to protect you and your family.

One year, we had a power outage here in Omaha due to a snowstorm. As a result, a lot of traffic lights were out. And when the traffic lights are out, you are supposed to treat them like four-way stops. Most people know this, but some don't. That night, someone almost hit me as he looked at his cell phone and drove right through the intersection. Fortunately, I was watching, but he could have easily killed or maimed people who were legally and rightfully going through that intersection.

If something like that were to happen and the distracted driver was uninsured or underinsured, the only protection you'd have would be this UM/UIM coverage. Remember that irresponsible people often have little or no coverage (or even just the minimum limits).

The bottom line: Look at your policy. Sit down with your agent and ask about this coverage. Ask about increasing your deductible to help offset cost. If possible, max out your UM/UIM coverage on your policy.

Chapter 3.

An Umbrella is Not Just for Rain

I think we can all agree that carrying an umbrella in our car is often helpful. But did you know that carrying Umbrella Coverage can literally save your life (or, at least, your lifestyle)?

If the unthinkable happens to you or your family, the economic harms and losses will quite often far exceed even the highest limits on a maxed-out UM/UIM coverage policy (what we discussed in the last chapter).

I've seen catastrophic injuries, brain injuries and paralysis; I've seen breadwinners killed or disabled to the point of no longer being able to provide for their families.

Take, for example, a 50-year-old man married for 20 years, with four kids at varying levels of education. They're all dependent on his income. And if he were to be killed or seriously injured, even if he had maximum coverage on UM/UIM—that family's loss is going to be greatly in excess of those limits.

So the next step would be to acquire an Umbrella Policy.

As the name indicates, it will be an "umbrella" or extra coverage on every policy you have. This covers home and auto, and adds an additional layer or depth of coverage. I have a $5 million umbrella that applies to both my auto and home policies.

You can buy an umbrella policy in coverages of $1 million plus increments. It is typically a requirement that you have a substantial amount of UM coverage before a carrier will sell you an umbrella policy. So be sure you follow the steps in Chapter 1 first.

In Nebraska, our limits are $25,000/$50,000 minimum for liability and UM coverage. If you go to your agent with just the minimum and then ask for a $3 million umbrella, the insurance company is not likely to sell you that umbrella policy unless you increase your coverage amount.

Again, if you go back to your property damage deductibles and try to increase those, it will put you in a better position to be able to max out coverage and will help you have funds for both an auto/home umbrella policy.

Remember that the legal system doesn't care about "fairness" and that the laws are all about some level of predictability. This means that anytime someone goes and buys any policy from an agent—the agent knows more about insurance policies than 99% of buyers.

And some of the main companies will sell umbrella policies; people will purchase these policies and believe they are providing protection for their family members as well, when these policies do nothing of the sort.

Unfortunately, no one reads a policy until *after* something bad happens. Then the policyholder discovers what really is or is not covered.

I had a case once where my clients had maxed-out coverage on their UM/UIM policy and bought a $2 million umbrella policy on top of that. They thought, in good faith, that they had protected their family.

When they got into a tragic accident, the other driver did not have adequate coverage. So my clients turned to their umbrella policy to help make up the difference, but the policy did not have coverage for family members.

How is this possible? Well, keep in mind that this was a 50-page policy. And when I read the policy, I found this clause buried in the bowels of the contract in a tiny paragraph that says the coverage "*does not* apply to you or family members."

That's the exact opposite of what my clients thought they were getting.

When they bought insurance from their agent, they asked for an umbrella policy. He gave it to them. Sadly enough, he only wanted that premium check or was either ignorant or less than honest.

And that clause is buried because the insurance company's actuaries know the statistics and that the odds of the injured party being the named insured or a family member are through the roof—so they bury that language on purpose.

I'll bet you're wondering what happened on this case? Well, the policy did state the fact that the insured and their family were not covered. It was there in black and white. Did it make sense? No. Was it fair? No. Was there anything we could do about it? No.

As lawyers, we have to pay attention to state law and supreme court rulings. The Nebraska Supreme Court would say, when addressed with these facts, that anytime parties enter into a contract (that's what buying insurance is—entering into a contract) we "presume" that both parties are on an equal playing field with regard to knowledge and power. In other words, both parties are presumed to have read and understood the policy. The court would presume that this family not only read it, but had the power to negotiate change.

More simply put, the court will act as if the father read and understood the policy in its entirety and had agreed that there wasn't going to be any coverage: that's the deal and he would have to live with it.

But the reality and truth of real life is that you are not ever on an equal playing field with insurance companies.

However, if the agent had said, "Here is our umbrella policy…" and then that father was informed enough to make certain it would provide coverage for himself and his family members by saying something like, "I want to see the part that specifically includes coverage for me and my family members." then maybe this story would have a happier ending.

Don't be afraid to ask questions and then verify, because there will be no recourse down the road. It's not right and it's not fair, but this is the way the courts work.

Your only protection here is that you are adamant that the agent shows you the coverage specifics. Write these down if you want to and make the agent prove the coverage is what you expect.

Never forget for one minute that the insurance company's objective is to make money. They are for-profit only. They want to pay out as little as they can.

And don't wait to be in a bad situation to find out the bad news. If you already own a policy like this, review it today and make sure you'll get what you're paying for, should the need ever arise.

And if you don't have a policy like this, be sure you get a good one that can provide the right coverage and peace of mind for you and your family down the line. Hopefully you'll never need it, but wouldn't it make you sleep better to know that you have it tucked away, just in case?

I know it makes me feel better.

Chapter 4.

Medical Pay Coverage

If you take a close look at your policy for something called Medical Pay Coverage, you may find that it doesn't exist in your current coverage. That's because this is a separate and unique coverage.

With this coverage, your insurance company will pay up to whatever limits you buy from them for medical bills for any person who is injured by occupying your car. Who is at fault is irrelevant.

The coverage will pay for anyone in your car, up to the limits of coverage, to cover the medical bills incurred by anyone who is in the car and injured as a result of an accident.

In other words, this will apply if you are at fault or if someone else is at fault. It's a great add-on bonus to a policy that can really be another life saver.

There are many people in today's America who either don't have health insurance or have insurance that isn't very good—where there is an enormous deductible. Are you one of these people?

Some policies have as much as $10,000 worth of deductibles that you must pay out of pocket before the insurer pays one cent of coverage.

And some people simply cannot even afford the premiums for the Affordable Healthcare Act.

Even if you do have health insurance, you'll find that it's a nightmare to get the insurer to pay the bills in a normal amount of time. My own staff spends hours corresponding with these insurance companies to get them to process claims for our clients—because medical providers expect to be paid.

In fact, medical providers have struggled with unpaid bills so often that they've taken an increasingly aggressive position with this matter. If your claim gets denied and you don't pay your balance within four to six months (or sometimes even less), it could be turned over to a collection agency. And this is even when you have health insurance!

This Med-Pay coverage becomes important because these insurers are much easier to deal with than health insurance companies. The turnaround time is far quicker and more reliable.

For clients who have Med-Pay coverage, we can write a letter to their company, and the company will forward a check to us. Then we can parse out the funds to the doctors' offices as needed.

To obtain this special Med-Pay coverage is not very expensive compared to collision and property coverage that is already on your policy. You can get it for as little as $1,000 worth of coverage, but I recommend $10,000 to $25,000.

This coverage provides a great cushion for your finances and helps to prevent stress (and bad credit reporting) should the need arise to use it.

Explore this coverage with your agent and look for a minimum of $10,000 worth. Remember that even small accidents with minimal injuries can cost as much as $6,000 to $8,000 in medical bills.

Chapter 5.

What is GAP Coverage?

Around 95% of my clients are driving a car that they still owe money on when the accident occurred. In fact, I'd say that most people are making payments on their cars as a general rule.

So, in this chapter, we're going to talk about something called "gap" coverage.

In a vast majority of states, as a result of successful insurance company lobbying, if someone runs a red light and totals your car—the liable person is only obligated to pay you the fair market value of the car.

What does this mean?

This means that if you just paid $5,000 for a new transmission and tires on your car but yet the car is valued by NADA or Kelly's Blue Book as being worth only $10,000, it doesn't matter that you just upgraded and invested in the car by $5,000 more than its face value—the insurer only has to pay the face value.

And what's worse...if you are making car payments but your car is worth a lesser value than the balance, then you'll be left owing the difference. You could easily find yourself upside down to the tune of thousands of dollars.

For example, you owe $14,000 on the car when the car is totaled. And the car's book value is only $10,000. You'd be left with a $4,000 loan balance due with no way to pay it. But, if you add gap coverage to your own policy, then that coverage would pick up the balance for you.

I recommend $10,000 gap coverage. It's not very expensive, and down the road it can help you solve a sticky situation.

SECTION TWO:

PREVENTION

Chapter 6.

The Rules of the Road

Always follow the rules of the road.

It sounds easy, but so many of us seem to take those rules for granted. The very rules that are put there to protect us are so often ignored, and so often this is why thousands of accidents occur every single day.

Posted Speed Limits

Speed limits exist for a reason. I have only a three-mile drive to work every day. It's a four-lane road with a posted 35 mph speed limit. Yet people are zipping past me left and right. Why? Why are we in such a hurry?

Accident reconstruction experts say that for every 10 mph you add to the vehicle's speed, the severity of injuries (should an accident occur) increases exponentially.

So, if someone is driving 55 mph versus 35 mph, the likelihood of a significant injury is doubled. And 80% of accidents involve at least one vehicle that is speeding.

Those speed limits are not just chosen at random. They've been posted based on research by engineers who are trying to safely control the flow of traffic.

Next time you're driving, watch for the posted speed limit and slow down.

Given certain weather conditions (snow, ice, rain, etc.), it is imperative to drive slower than the speed limit in order to be safe. Don't think that just because you could driver faster that you should drive faster.

Following Too Closely

It is a proven fact that a human's perception/reaction time is about three seconds. Given that fact, driving only one car length behind the car in front of you is simply not enough.

Leave yourself a safe following distance. Count the seconds between you and the car in front as it passes by a stationary object (such as a lamp post or mail box).

The time you'll need to safely apply the brakes is more than you think. And braking early is crucial to performing an easy or controlled stop.

Obey Traffic Signals

If a traffic light turns yellow, I look to see if I have enough time to bring the car to a safe, controlled stop. Remember, you are allowed to drive through yellow only if you are so close to the intersection that you would not be able to safely bring your car to a stop.

Most people don't know (or don't care) that it is against the law to accelerate through a yellow light.

Impaired or Distracted Driving

You should never drive after consuming alcohol and/or drugs. Most people would take offense at my telling them that because it is obvious. But even talking on a handheld phone has the equivalent distractive effect of having three cocktails or beers.

And did you know that drivers who are texting experience the same effect as someone who has had six to 12 alcoholic beverages?

My paralegal's husband is a construction site supervisor for road construction and often works on the highways. He says that he's seen people on laptops while they are driving! Can you believe this?

I once tried a case for the wrongful death of a 15-year-old girl. The driver of the truck that hit her was distracted and went off the road, hitting a disabled car because he wasn't paying attention.

It's tragedies such as these that should prove the point I'm making. Yet we see it happening every single day.

Sometimes I purposefully take back roads because I'm so acutely aware of fast-moving traffic and the dangers of the roadways.

People take the fundamental rules of road for granted, and these rules are just as easily forgotten by older drivers, too.

Always have respect for traffic control. It is there for a reason, and it could save your life.

Never Trust Other Drivers

People come in to see me after they've been in an accident, and they say things like, "But I was in a crosswalk." Or "I had the green light!"

It just doesn't matter. These days, you have to watch the road, drive defensively, and anticipate anything that could happen. Because once that tragedy has occurred, it's too late to argue the point.

You could cherry-pick any 10 cases that I've handled for families who've experienced a tragic accident—people for whom I've been able to recover huge verdicts or settlements. And if you asked them if they'd rather have their arm back or their child back or the pain-free use of their body back, they'd all take that over any amount of money.

There is just no value you can really put on the quality of life. Our legal system is not able to provide adequate compensation for people who have suffered devastating losses.

It just doesn't add up. When we are talking about the legal system, we try to do the best we can to get adequate compensation for the losses our clients have suffered. We look at the value we attached to a loved one, and we somehow have to reduce that to money. What can we get for you to cover medical needs or financial needs?

But I've never seen an outcome that really set things right.

The point is that it doesn't matter if you had the right of way or were on the crosswalk minding your own business. No one can set things right. The bottom line here is to never trust other drivers.

Act as if the other drivers are going to violate the rules.

When the light turns green, does that mean go? No! It means when the light turns green, you have the qualified right to enter the intersection only if it is clear.

I had a case where a wonderful lady—a hardworking mother and physics teacher—is on her way home from work one day. She takes the bus and then needs to cross the busy intersection to get to her house. She pushes the crosswalk button, waits for the light and begins to cross. But the light wasn't timed correctly. It didn't give her enough time to cross at a normal walking speed.

That was when a 35-year-old man (a distracted driver) saw that the light was green in the intersection up ahead and never slowed down. He just flew right on through and hit this innocent lady. She was thrown 45 feet through the air and sustained major injuries.

Green does not always mean go.

Chapter 7.

If an Accident Occurs

What do you do if you are in an accident?

Sometimes accidents happen, and it is best to know the first few steps that are crucial should this happen to you.

❶ Call 911 any time you are in a wreck.

Sometimes people assume that someone else has called 911. Don't worry about that. You call immediately. Don't assume.

❷ Depending upon where the wreck occurs—if it is on an interstate or in heavy traffic—you should assess the situation to see if you need to get out of the line of traffic.

Most officials will tell you that you should stay in your car, unless there is smoke/fire or major damage.

❸ In the event that you are injured and need medical attention, ask for help when you call 911.

In the event that you or someone in your car has been injured, the police are frequently going to call an ambulance. As a general rule of thumb, go ahead and accept that.

If you have transportation and someone can pick you up, it is a good idea to get checked out in the emergency room. In cases of minor injuries, your body will be flooded with adrenaline and you may not really realize you're hurt. So it is always better to get checked out anyway.

Obviously, if it is a serious accident, you will be carted off in an ambulance.

Later, if your case involves legal action, the at-fault driver's insurance company will be looking carefully at these first treatment records—trying to rip holes in it. It is a sad commentary, but that's how it works.

➍ When you see the doctor, give a thorough response to all of his or her questions.

During your visit, the doctor will complete something called a Patient Medical Narrative History.

In medical school, doctors are taught to document everything that the patient tells them in the chart. In this day and age, doctors will dictate notes between patients as they race from room to room—that dictation goes to a transcriptionist, and it becomes part of the patient chart. But in medical school doctors were told, "If it is not in the chart—it didn't happen."

So if you tell the doctor you're having pain in your neck and back but you forget to mention to the doctor that you are not able to get out of a chair because of the pain—it won't end up in your chart.

Before you see the doctor, do a systems review from top to bottom of your body. Watch the ways in which your pain is affecting your everyday life and share this with the doctor. The doctor needs to hear all this information to make the proper recommendation for your treatment and recovery.

The doctor's primary goal is for the patient to make a full recovery or the best recovery the patient can possibly make. To give the doctors the best chance of helping you do this, you need to share with them as much detailed information as you can.

It is really important to be a good historian. Tell the doctor everything. Give the doctor some sense of what transpired—give the narrative of what happened in the wreck and then bring the doctor up to date on your injuries and pain and how they affect you in your day-to-day life.

At some point in the process, you'll either make a full recovery or the doctor will say, "This is as good as we can get you."

If you're my client, after you complete your treatment, I'll eventually be having a face-to-face meeting with your doctor. To pursue your case, we'll need a medical/legal opinion letter where the doctor sets forth the nature and extent of the patient's injuries. But we can't get a full opinion without the doctor going back and reviewing your chart…the chart that you've helped the doctor create from the first day of the accident (or your first visit) up until this point by clearly communicating all the details of your injury.

We'll be asking the doctor all sort of questions, like:

- What is the nature of this diagnosis?
- Is this injury consistent with this type of wreck or impact?
- Do you have an opinion as to whether the treatment was made necessary by the wreck?
- Did the injury cause the patient to miss substantial time from work?
- Is the injury going to leave the patient with any remaining problems?

We need to have opinions from the doctors that clearly summarize your diagnosis, or you cannot make a claim for it in an injury case. Everything is evaluated against the backdrop of a courtroom.

You cannot make a claim without a medical expert who offers sworn opinions under oath. The expert must believe the wreck caused this injury, disability, or problem.

I bring this up because doctors view a patient's chart as a sort of sacred text. If something is not in the chart, it didn't happen. Every time you go to the doctor, you need to remember to tell your doctor everywhere you are hurting as well as how it is affecting you in your daily life. Tell everything.

Doctors have hundred/thousands of patients and they need to review the chart to remember everything to recollect your case.

If you end up filing a lawsuit, it can be weeks or months after treatment before an attorney will be involved or consulting with the doctor. Sometimes it takes that long to receive a full diagnosis or know what the result of the treatment will be.

So, if you go to the doctor, tell him or her every detail of how you are hurting and how it is affecting you. Ask the doctor what you can do to get better.

Then follow the doctor's direction perfectly. If you see the doctor twice and he or she recommends six physical therapies, and you cancel follow-up appointments and don't complete the physical therapies—the doctor is not going to be very inclined to help your case down the road. When the lawyer asks for a report from the doctor, it is going to say, "The patient didn't do half the things I recommended."

If this happens. then we have nothing to discuss with the doctor, because we have no support from the doctor.

Bottom line: the most important thing that a client can do to help us look out for him or her is to be a good patient. Follow medical advice. If the doctor tells you that you should do it, then do it.

Don't be the tough guy. Tell the doctor everything up front. Do what your medical providers tell you to do. Protect yourself.

If people follow these suggestions, it will help protect them later. As the saying goes, "An ounce of prevention is worth a pound of cure."

Chapter 8.

Young Drivers

Having specialized in this field for 30 years now, you begin to see patterns. One of the things I've seen is that younger drivers are a great risk to themselves and others on the roadway, and statistics confirm it.

Young drivers are defined as drivers under the age of 20 years old. Did you know that teens are four times more likely to crash than drivers over 30? And the most common cause of death of youths ages 13-19 is car accidents?

In fact, over 50% of teens talk on the phone when they are driving. For each passenger in the car driven by a teenager, the risk of an accident increases.

How about all those statistics to make you a worried parent?

Most crashes occur between midnight and 3:00 a.m. because young people are driving for recreational purposes during these times. That is when they are more likely to be using alcohol or drugs and more likely to be speeding due to peer pressure.

Here's a quote attributed to Henry Ford: "There is no substitute for experience." And what better place does this hold true than with regard to teen drivers?

The truth is that teen drivers have virtually no experience. They don't fully understand how cars respond to braking or cornering, or how the application of brakes can be radically affected by things like your direction, cornering, weather, etc.

Most adult drivers haven't attended a professional driving school, but they do have hundreds or thousands of hours behind the wheel. Teens don't have this experience yet.

Small things that we take for granted, like how quickly that oncoming vehicle is going to close in on you when you're considering making that left-hand turn in front of traffic, are new to a teen driver. At least, as an adult, you have a sense of what is safe.

Neurological studies confirm that the brains development of younger people (teens) are not fully developed. So what can you do to help establish them as safer, more aware drivers?

I recommend enrolling teens in driving school. I know that most students take some form of Driver's Ed in high school. It includes education classroom time and driving time. But, truthfully, this is limited training.

You should definitely consider seeking out a real driving school for your teen. AAA offers driver training; Tire

Rack, BMW, and local car groups do as well. These Performance Driving Schools will pair your teen with a professional driver in a one-on-one driving experience.

Your teen will need a helmet and a headset so the instructor/passenger can speak through it into the driver's ear. Most schools provide this equipment.

That one-on-one time with an expert driver is invaluable It's one thing to tell someone and it's another to show someone, but this real-time coaching experience will make all the difference.

The men and women who teach these classes are driving enthusiasts. They will show young drivers what it is like to go off road and lose control of the car. The experience of going off the track and into the dirt under controlled conditions will make the student a better prepared driver in the real world.

At 35 years of age I took one of these classes. I came away from that experience a far more cautious driver because I now had a profound appreciation for the dangers that surround every car on the road. Curbs, trees, and light posts are just a few of the things that could lead to catastrophic injury should you lose control of your vehicle.

The net result of someone going to a Performance Driving School is not that they are now driving the streets thinking they are Mario Andretti, but they will have that knowledge and experience and know what it feels like to lose control and will understand how seemingly innocuous objects (other drivers, trees, curbs, mailbox, etc.) can be incredibly dangerous.

For this small investment, you will have a driver who is far more likely to survive his or her teen years and have a long, safe, wonderful life

I appreciate that we all struggle with money, but this is an investment you cannot afford not to make.

Another couple of recommendations:

❶ There are technology phone blocks you can put on cell phones through your provider. If the car is moving, the phone will not ring or notify the driver if someone calls or texts. The phone will send out an "I'm driving" message automatically.

❷ Newer cars have telematics systems that will record all the information about the vehicle: where the vehicle is, how fast it was moving, fuel consumption, the speed it drove, if any hard brakes were made during the trip. You can use this to monitor your teens in the car.

❸ Enforce strict rules—no passengers allowed.

❹ Add governors to the car to help control speed.

Chapter 9.

Alert and Aware

What if you see a collision coming?

You've followed all the rules and a collision is coming your way by no fault of your own. If this happens, chances are that you'll have only a couple of seconds to realize that impact is coming. You probably won't be able to do much of anything.

But hopefully you are wearing your seatbelt. The most important safety tip anyone could ever offer—buckle up!

Most modern cars have headrests, and it is a good thing to be sitting upright. If you have a headrest, put your head up against it. During a collision your head will snap forward and back but start with it against the headrest, if possible.

Don't try to brace for impact. I know this will be hard to do, but relaxing and holding the steering wheel at the

10:00/2:00 position is the best thing you can do. Keep your arms straight. Don't bend or twist your wrists.

Most cars come equipped with air bags, and if there is an impact—let the air bag do its work.

And, most importantly, don't try to avoid the wreck by swerving. You can cause far worse problems by swerving. This can cause a change of trajectory that could be much more serious.

Chapter 10.

A Bird's-Eye View

I hope you've found this book helpful. It has been my intention to share some brief tips with you that will hopefully help you to protect yourself and prevent some issue that could occur in your busy life on the road.

I'd like to close out the book with a Bird's-Eye View of the process—a timeline of events for you if you're ever injured in a wreck.

When I meet with clients or potential clients, they are always concerned about what's going to happen next.

No one ever expects that they will be hurt. And if the accident itself is not stressful enough, then they also come to discover that they are involved in our adversarial legal process. In this country, we'd like to think that the two sides go to war and the truth comes out. But this is not exactly what happens, unfortunately.

You have great concerns about your health and well-being. What if you can't work due to pain, or a family member is hurt? How are you going to make ends meet, pay medical bills, or get treatment?

These are all valid concerns. But then, you have claims adjusters from the insurer of the person at fault, and they're calling and pestering you and wanting statements and paperwork.

Everything becomes overwhelming. So, when people come in to sit down with me, I'll listen to everything they tell me about their accident and what happened to them. I may conclude that they don't need a lawyer, or that it's too soon to tell.

But even the people who clearly need a lawyer become calmer and more relaxed after I give them this overview.

So here's what I'd like to share with you, and what I share with everyone I meet with.

I think it is a good idea that everyone who is involved in a crash contact someone like me to get a list of dos and don'ts.

If there's been a death or serious injury, most people understand out of the gate that they will need an attorney.

I'm convinced that I can put someone who has had these type of injuries in a better financial position because they have hired me.

And there are other cases where people have injuries, but it is harder to tell if they will need an attorney. But the sooner they talk to someone like me, the better off they will be.

If I'm not confident that I can put them in a better position—if their injuries are not going to have enough critical weight—there is no reason to hire me. For instance, if you have an injury that is better in three months, you won't need me.

But if you have a death or major loss, then a personal injury attorney can make a huge difference in your life.

After having done this for 30 years, I would happily spend a good chunk of my day talking with people who have been injured or have a loved one who has been injured. If it's not clear whether or not you need a lawyer, at least let me give you some notes.

So, if you want to, you can try to handle a serious injury case on your own. You have a right to do so. But you will lose ground in the end.

If you have a sore neck and are better in 2 months, it's not a problem.

But if this goes on for a long time and you have not met with someone like me, you will fall behind. If you have not been keeping documentation and other things you should have been doing, you could find a tough road ahead of you.

We settle 90% of cases, but they are all set against the backdrop of what would happen if we went to court.

There are nuances and difficulties that occur in the adversarial legal system, and you just need a lawyer to help you see how it all works.

Here are the general stages through which these cases go from the moment a drunk driver crashes into your car and your wife and daughter are injured.

Be mindful of documentation. You'd be surprised how many at-fault drivers say, "Don't call police, let's handle ourselves." But always call the police and get a report. Always!

You need documentation; let them record everything.

Next, police officers are busy, and they are running from call to call. Frequently people appear after the wreck and say they saw it or witnessed it. The police may not get their names/numbers.

If this happens, be mindful to get names and numbers and keep them for later use, if needed. Everybody has a phone with camera; get photographs of the scene and the vehicles and witnesses, if you can.

Typically, when the police come and see that you've been hurt, they will offer to call an ambulance. It is best to take them up on such an offer. In the alternative, have someone you know come pick you up and take you to the emergency room so you can get checked out.

Go to the doctor the same day and tell the doctor everything so they can document your injury was caused by a wreck. Be a good historian—explain where you are hurting and how it is affecting you. Give a good patient history—detailed and straightforward.

They need to understand and recommend the best possible treatment.

The number-one overarching goal is to make a complete medical recovery, or as good a recovery as possible. You need to be detailed when describing your symptoms to the doctor so they can give you their best medical skills and recommendations.

Do what the doctor tells you to do. Follow the instructions completely. Whether you need a lawyer or not, at some point, the claims adjuster will be looking at these records and trying to find ways in which they can question your compliance with the doctors' orders or other ways to minimize the claim so the insurance company can hold on to more of the money that should rightfully be going to you.

The reason we pay premiums is to get protection, but insurance companies are for profit. They keep the adjusters and the salespeople in different buildings in order to keep their motives separate. Their profit is based upon how little money they pay on claims and how much they charge for the same policy.

Insurers know that a jury will look unfavorably on a person who doesn't follow a doctor's instructions. On the flip side, a jury will feel favorable toward you if you try hard to get better and follow your treatment plan.

My suggestion is that anybody who has been involved in a wreck and required medical treatment as a result should call an attorney just to touch base.

The at-fault driver's company is going to contact you immediately to get a medical authorization signed by you. You may think they are offering to pay medical bills. What they actually want is to obtain your medical records—even those created before the wreck—so they can go through all of your health history. They are not going to pay your bills as they come in. Remember, it is an adversarial process. If the at-fault driver's company were to pay bills as you incurred them, they would be in effect helping you document and build a claim against them, which would require them to pay out more money.

When asked to sign a medical authorization, people think the at-fault driver's insurance company means "sign this and then we can help you." This is a very common misunderstanding. Never sign these. If someone comes to see me and they have already done this, I will send a letter to revoke it.

In my career, I've seen these companies attempt to get complete past medical records on victims to try to reduce the claim. I've also seen them write letters to your own treating doctor implying that they are writing on your behalf as if they represent you and asking the doctor to confirm that you're completely recovered.

These requests are trying to steer the doctor to minimize your claim and injuries.

If you have medical pay coverage (as we discussed earlier) with your own insurance carrier, your carrier may ask for this same type of release, and that's fine. Don't worry about that. They'll need the authorization to get your bills paid. Just know to whom you're talking.

If it is a serious case and you're in the hospital, I will meet with you and get releases and a contract, and then we will send letters on your behalf telling the insurance carriers that they are to speak only to us. We will not allow our client to speak with anyone who is possibly in an adversarial position.

Our staff ensures bills are being paid (to prevent collections and credit issues); we want our clients to focus on getting better.

Clients ask, "How long this will take?" We don't know. "You can't push the river" is a Native American saying, and it certainly holds true for the legal system.

It could be six months to a year or more of medical treatment. We need to know the doctor's full diagnosis and treatment plan. We have to wait until we get to that point to obtain a good medical opinion. We have to know how your injury is going to impact you in the long term.

We need a full evaluation to estimate the true value of your claim. Until you get to that point, we will stay in touch with you regarding your progress, keeping our finger on the pulse of treatment.

When you complete treatment, I will make an appointment with the doctors to get narrative medical and legal reports. Then I will meet with the doctor to discuss what would be his or her possible testimony.

Once we have bills and records, we ask the clients to come in and discuss the case. Then I will write a demand letter to the opposing insurance company.

I'll ask the insurer to name the largest amount of money they will put on the table to avoid having to go to court. After some back-and-forth communication, the insurance company will tell us what is the largest offer they are willing to pay voluntarily. At that point, I will call my clients in and present the offer to them.

I'll give the advice to my clients that I would give to my own family members. I'll explain the offer, and give them my considered opinion as to whether it makes sense to accept the offer or to file suit. In laying all of this out for the client, I'll give them some sense of what a likely jury verdict range might be, and why. I'll give them an idea of what a trial would cost and how long a trial would be.

I'll let my clients know how we have to pay for expert testimony. Is it a smart gamble to try the case or not? And I'll make a recommendation, but the client has to make the ultimate decision.

I give my clients my best considered advice, and I take this seriously. There have been a number of times where I've suggested settling a case, and my clients chose to go to court. I'm happy to do that, but I've put them in a position to make the wisest decision possible.

So far, every time I've told my clients that we may get less from a jury, but I think we should try the case because the offer is too low—we've ended up with a better outcome. But our clients need the best advice I can give them.

I'm a tour guide on the tour you never wanted to take. I take pride on the reviews we've been given. We've analyzed tragic circumstances and taken all the actions necessary to help our clients and their family members.

In the event we have to file suit because we don't have a reasonable offer from a carrier, we work to achieve the best outcome for our clients. Sometimes we are able to settle a case before it goes to trial. Most people have a lot of fear about going to court and moving forward.

If we don't have a serious offer, sometimes just filing the lawsuit will push the carrier to a better offer. It sends a message that we are not willing to back down.

Once the lawsuit has been filed, the insurer will have to involve its own attorney to follow through with an answer to our claim and to issue written discovery (this is a series of Q&A between parties). It allows the company to conduct its own investigation and allows us to prove that we do have a valid claim.

At this point, depositions will often be scheduled. These are face-to-face meetings held on the record (typically in our offices), and both sides ask questions. I am present in all of my clients' depositions, and I will spend a lot of time preparing you for this. My goal is for you to be comfortable and eager to tell the truth.

A deposition allows the other side to check and verify that you didn't have a lot of prior problems before the injury. It allows them to meet you, to see that you are likable and that a jury will most certainly like you.

At this point, the insurer often reevaluates the claim and makes another offer.

Insurance companies don't want to go to court. It's expensive, and there is a good likelihood of a high jury verdict.

But, if your case does go to court, it is typically 12-18 months after your injury occurred. This is a significant length of time, but there is a lot of preparation involved so that we can present the case to the best of our ability.

Under our legal system, you have "one bite of apple." If you settle or get a verdict, but then have second thoughts—you don't get to go back later. We must do it right the first time. It is serious to present a case to a jury. A good attorney is mindful of the fact that a jury verdict is going to have to take care of the client for the rest of his or her life.

If this is a permanent life-changing injury, it is vital that the jury hears all of the evidence that they need to hear. You are asking a group of 12 regular people to take in a lot of information and then return a just verdict. It is a significant undertaking for everyone involved.

And that's a bird's-eye view of the whole process from start to finish. I can assure you that a lawsuit isn't always necessary. And I can also assure you that a lawyer, like me, isn't always necessary either.

But isn't it nice to know what you can do to help protect yourself in case the need arises?

I hope you've found something here that reassures you, comforts you, or simply educates you.

Don't forget, it's always better to be safe than sorry.

About the Author

Matt Miller is a native of Omaha, Nebraska, and is a graduate of Creighton University and Creighton Law School. He began his legal career working for one of the area's premier personal injury lawyers. Matt's early success in the courtroom led to a job with an insurance defense law firm, where he defended cases on behalf of insurance companies. Disillusioned with attaining favorable results for large corporations in cases involving accident victims, Matt "switched sides" and vowed to work on behalf of injured people from that point forward. His insurance defense experience has given him great insight in combatting the tactics used by insurance companies. Matt has built his career sharing the truth with jurors about his clients' injuries and the impact of those injuries on their lives, and by countering the tactics used by insurance companies to distort the truth.

Matt has been recognized as one of The Best Lawyers in America, The Top 100 of The National Trial Lawyers of America, and Omaha Magazine's Best of Omaha since 2007.

Made in the USA
Monee, IL
04 November 2026

67387335R10036